FIVE SHORT PLAYS

Stage 1

It's not always easy to know the right thing to do. For the people in these five short plays, life can be difficult and sometimes very funny.

Harry and his friends are fed up because they haven't got any money. But Harry has a plan to change all this. It's a good plan, but even the best plans can go badly wrong . . .

'Listen,' says Ron, 'My friend over there has got a gun. Give me the money! Give it to me now!'

'What money?' the woman answers. 'I'm sorry, this is not a bank. This is a library.'

Sid and Ron must steal something, but it isn't easy to rob a library. The woman happily gives them library cards so they can borrow books, and not steal them. In fact, she's very pleased to help . . .

Things are often more difficult than they seem. But as in all these plays, people are often more interesting, and much funnier, when they're trying to do the right thing.

Martyn Ford, the author of these plays, is a writer, teacher, actor and illustrator, who lives and works in Brighton, on the south coast of England.

OXFORD BOOKWORMS PLAYSCRIPTS
Series Editor: Clare West

OXFORD BOOKWORMS

For a full list of titles in all the Oxford Bookworms series,
please refer to the *Oxford English* catalogue.

OXFORD BOOKWORMS PLAYSCRIPTS

Stage 1

The Butler Did It and Other Plays
Bill Bowler (retold by Clare West)

A Ghost in Love and Other Plays
Michael Dean

The Murder of Mary Jones
Tim Vicary

Sherlock Holmes: Two Plays
Sir Arthur Conan Doyle (retold by John Escott)

Stage 2

The Importance of Being Earnest
Oscar Wilde (retold by Susan Kingsley)

Much Ado About Nothing
William Shakespeare (retold by Alistair McCallum)

One Thousand Dollars and Other Plays
O. Henry (retold by John Escott)

Romeo and Juliet
William Shakespeare (retold by Alistair McCallum)

MARTYN FORD

Five Short Plays

OXFORD UNIVERSITY PRESS

OXFORD
UNIVERSITY PRESS

Great Clarendon Street, Oxford OX2 6DP

Oxford University Press is a department of the University of Oxford.
It furthers the University's objective of excellence in research, scholarship,
and education by publishing worldwide in

Oxford New York

Auckland Cape Town Dar es Salaam Hong Kong Karachi
Kuala Lumpur Madrid Melbourne Mexico City Nairobi
New Delhi Shanghai Taipei Toronto

With offices in

Argentina Austria Brazil Chile Czech Republic France Greece
Guatemala Hungary Italy Japan Poland Portugal Singapore
South Korea Switzerland Thailand Turkey Ukraine Vietnam

OXFORD and OXFORD ENGLISH are registered trade marks of
Oxford University Press in the UK and in certain other countries

ISBN-13: 978 0 19 423218 0
ISBN-10: 0 19 423218 2

Printed in Hong Kong

ACKNOWLEDGEMENT
Illustrated by: Rob Davis

CONTENTS

INTRODUCTION

This play is about a group of five friends. They are fed up because they haven't got any money. But this is all going to change soon. One of the group, Harry, has a plan – a very good plan.

CHARACTERS IN THE PLAY

Harry
Sid
Wilf
Gladys
Ron
Three people reading in a library
Woman working in a library

PERFORMANCE NOTES

Scene 1: A room in the friends' home. There are chairs and a table. Everything looks very old and dirty. Wilf and Gladys are drinking tea. Ron is looking out of the window. Sid is watching the television, but it is not working.

Scene 2: Inside a library. There is a woman sitting at a table. She works in the library. Three other people are standing or sitting, holding books in their hands and reading.

You will need a table, chairs, an old television, two library cards and some books.

The Robbery

The plan

Harry comes into the room. His friends look up at him.

HARRY Hello, everyone. What are you doing?

SID Nothing, Harry, nothing! What can we do? We haven't got any money.

HARRY I know, I know. But it's OK. I have some work for us. We can make a lot of money.

WILF Work? But you don't like work, Harry.

HARRY Ah, but this work is different.

GLADYS How, Harry? What are we going to do?

HARRY We're going to rob a bank.

GLADYS Rob a bank? But how can we?

HARRY I have a plan, a very good plan.

WILF Which bank are we going to rob?

HARRY The Capital Bank.

WILF Which one is that?

HARRY The one next to the library in the High Street.

SID That's a very big bank!

HARRY Be quiet and listen. Now, I want Wilf to drive the car, and Gladys to stand outside the bank and watch the street.

'I have a plan, a very good plan.'

WILF AND GLADYS   OK, Harry.

HARRY   Sid—

SID   (*Excitedly*) Yes, Harry? What do you want me to do?

HARRY   You must go into the bank and speak to everyone there. Say to them, 'Stay there! Don't move! I've got a gun in my pocket.'

SID   But Harry, we haven't got a gun.

HARRY   I know that! You just put your hand in your pocket like this. Move your hand up and down in your pocket and say, 'This is a gun!'

SID   I understand.

HARRY   Good. Now, Ron, I want you to go with Sid—

RON   Yes, Harry, and then what?

HARRY   Go to one of the bank workers and say, 'My friend has a gun. Give me the money!'

GLADYS What are *you* going to do, Harry?

HARRY   I'm going to wait in the car with Wilf. Do you have any questions?

ALL   No.

HARRY   OK. So let's look at the plan again . . .

SCENE 2
The robbery

Sid and Ron run into the library. The people there look up from their books.

SID   Listen to me, all of you. This is a robbery. Don't move. I've got a gun in my pocket.

PEOPLE Oh, don't shoot! Please don't shoot! We don't want to die.

SID   Nobody's going to die, but you must do what I say. (*To Ron*) Go on, Ron. What are you waiting for? Get the money! Quick!

Ron goes over to the woman who works there.

RON   Listen, my friend over there has got a gun. Give me the money! Give it to me now!

WOMAN What money?

RON What do you mean, 'What money?' The money in this bank, of course!

WOMAN I'm sorry, this is not a bank. This is a library.

RON What did you say – a library?

WOMAN That's right. People come here to borrow books. We don't have any money here.

RON Er, you don't have any money . . . Oh dear! . . . Sid! Sid!

SID What? Have you got the money?

RON There isn't any money. It's not a bank, Sid. We're not in a bank. This is a library!

SID A library?

RON That's right. They've only got books – lots and lots of books!

SID Books? Well, get some of those, then. We must take something, or Harry's going to be angry.

RON (*To the woman*) Give me lots of books!

WOMAN Have you got a library card?

RON A card? No, I haven't.

WOMAN I'm sorry, you can't borrow books without a library card.

RON Look, you don't understand, we're not *borrowing* books, we're *stealing* them!

WOMAN I'm sorry, but you can't do that.

RON Sid, we can't steal books, she says.

'Have you got a library card?'

SID   I've got a gun. Tell her that!

RON   My friend's got a gun and he knows how to shoot!

WOMAN Look, it's not a problem. I can give you and your friend a library card. Then you can borrow the books and not steal them. What are your names?

RON   Oh, all right. I'm Ronald Savage, and he's Sidney Dupree.

WOMAN (*Writing*) Ronald Savage . . . Sidney Dupree. And what's your address?

RON   27 Dunfore Road, Hamley.

WOMAN (*Writing*) 27 Dunfore Road, Hamley. Good, here
       you are. (*She gives Ron two library cards*.) Now
       you can borrow some books.

RON   But I don't know anything about reading. You
       must help me. Which books are best?

SID   Quick, Ron! I can't stand here much longer.

WOMAN Here are some good books for you. (*She takes
       three books from the shelves*.) *The Great Train
       Robbery*, *The Return of Sherlock Holmes*, and
       The Adventures of Robin Hood. They're all very
       famous books.

RON   Oh, that's nice. They look interesting. Thanks.

SID   Ron, come on! Quick!

RON   It's OK, Sid, I've got the books.

SID   All right. (*To the people in the library*) We're
       going now, but don't move. Don't move or talk
       for five minutes.

PERSON 1   Can we read?

SID   Er, all right. But you must read *quietly*, OK?

RON   Come on, Sid! Let's go. Harry and the others are
       waiting.

WOMAN Goodbye, and happy reading!

RON   Oh yes, thank you. All right, Sid. I'm coming.

They run out of the library.

PERSON 2   Oh dear! I was so afraid!

6

WOMAN   Oh, they weren't so bad. The one called Sid – he didn't really have a gun, you know.

PERSON 3   Perhaps. But they were robbers. They wanted to rob the bank!

WOMAN   (*Laughing*) Yes, but they came into the wrong building!

PERSON 1   Why do you look so pleased?

WOMAN   Well, it's important for everybody to read books – not just you and me, but *everybody* . . . even bank robbers!

PERSON 2   But you aren't going to get those books back, are you?

WOMAN   Oh yes, I am. Remember, I've got their names and their address!

'Remember, I've got their names and their address!'

INTRODUCTION

In this play a man is lying in the street. Three different people stop and look. Perhaps the man needs help. But they don't know him, so it's not their problem, is it? Then a woman in blue arrives and suddenly things are different.

CHARACTERS IN THE PLAY

Patrick
Rebecca
David
Woman in blue
Michael Scott, a man lying in the street
Doctor
Nurse

PERFORMANCE NOTES

For this play you will need a small bottle of pills, a glass of water, blue clothes for the woman, a white coat for the doctor, and perhaps special clothes for the nurse.

The Right Thing to Do

A man is lying in the street. Rebecca is walking past. She stops and looks at him, then she looks around her – there is nobody there. She starts to walk away, stops, and goes back to look at the man again. Patrick walks past and stops to look at the man.

PATRICK What's the matter with him?

REBECCA I don't know.

PATRICK Is he dead?

REBECCA No, he's alive, I think.

PATRICK Are you going to help him?

'Is he dead?'

9

REBECCA Me? Why me?

PATRICK You were here first.

REBECCA Yes, I was, but—

David comes in.

DAVID What's the matter with him?

PATRICK We don't know.

DAVID He looks ill.

REBECCA His eyes are closed. Look!

DAVID Perhaps he's asleep.

REBECCA Asleep? In the street?

PATRICK Wake him up then.

DAVID Why me? You do it.

PATRICK (*To Rebecca*) What about you?

REBECCA Me?

PATRICK Yes. You were here first.

REBECCA Yes, but it's not my problem.

DAVID And it's not my problem!

A woman in blue comes in. She kneels down at once to help the man.

REBECCA Hey, what are you doing?

WOMAN I'm helping this man, of course!

DAVID Are you a doctor?

WOMAN No, I'm not, but he needs help.

REBECCA Do you know him?

WOMAN No, I don't.

REBECCA Then he's not your problem.

'Go and call an ambulance.'

WOMAN Oh, be quiet!

REBECCA (*To the others*) Did you hear that? She said, 'Be quiet!'

WOMAN Be quiet and help.

REBECCA She said it again!

WOMAN (*To David*) Go and call an ambulance.

DAVID Me?

WOMAN Yes, you. And be quick.

DAVID But—

WOMAN Be quick! (*David goes away.*) Now you – (*turning to Rebecca*) go and get some water.

REBECCA Where from?

WOMAN From that house over there. Don't look at me like that. Go!

REBECCA I'm going. (*Rebecca goes away.*)

WOMAN (*To Patrick*) Feel his pulse.

PATRICK But I—

WOMAN Go on! Feel his pulse.

PATRICK (*Kneeling down and taking the man's pulse*) Well, he's still alive. He's saying something!

WOMAN What is he saying?

PATRICK He said, 'Pills,' I think.

WOMAN (*To Patrick*) Pills? Look in his pocket.

PATRICK I can't do that!

WOMAN Look in his pocket!

Patrick looks in the man's coat pocket.

PATRICK There's a bottle with some writing on it.

WOMAN What does it say? Read it!

PATRICK It says, 'For the heart. If you feel ill, take one of these pills.'

Rebecca comes back with a glass of water.

REBECCA I've got the water.

WOMAN Good. (*To Patrick*) Give him one of the pills with some water.

Patrick helps the man to sit up. He gives him a pill and some water.

MAN (*Very quietly*) Thank you, thank you!

PATRICK How do you feel?

MAN A little better now.

The woman in blue goes away. The others do not see this. David comes running back.

DAVID   The ambulance is coming.

PATRICK   Good.

DAVID   How is he?

REBECCA   He's feeling a little better.

A doctor and a nurse come in. Patrick stands up.

DOCTOR   (*Kneeling down by the man*) What's the matter?

MAN   I was ill. It was my heart. That man gave me one of my pills. I'm all right now.

The doctor and the nurse help him to stand up.

NURSE   What's your name?

MAN   Scott. Michael Scott.

DOCTOR   Michael Scott, the famous TV chef?

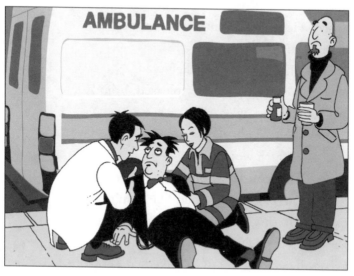

'What's the matter?'

13

MAN Yes, that's right.

NURSE Come with us, Mr Scott. We'd like to take you to hospital.

MAN But I feel better now.

NURSE Perhaps, but you must go to hospital.

MAN All right. (*Turning to the others*) Well, thank you very much, everybody.

DAVID That's all right.

REBECCA We're happy to help.

PATRICK Get well soon.

MAN Thank you again. Goodbye!

The doctor and the nurse help Scott to walk away.

REBECCA He's alive, and he's going to be OK.

PATRICK He's alive because we were here.

DAVID Michael Scott—

REBECCA The famous TV chef!

PATRICK We can all feel very pleased, I think.

REBECCA Oh yes, we can.

DAVID What about the woman?

REBECCA Which woman?

DAVID The woman who helped. Where is she?

PATRICK Oh, *her*! I remember. She didn't help *us*.

DAVID 'Do this, do that,' she said. 'Be quick!'

REBECCA She said, 'Be quiet,' to me.

PATRICK That's right. I didn't like her. Did you?

REBECCA No, I didn't. Where is she now?

'Well done, everybody!'

PATRICK She walked away.

DAVID That's right – she just walked away. She didn't want to help.

REBECCA We did everything.

DAVID Yeah. Everything.

PATRICK Today was an important day for us.

DAVID It was. We helped someone famous.

REBECCA Because of us he didn't die.

DAVID We were there for him.

PATRICK It was the right thing to do.

REBECCA Yes, it was. Well done, everybody!

DAVID (*To Rebecca*) And well done to *you*—

PATRICK Well done to all of us!

INTRODUCTION

This play is about a young person who wants to change his life. Chris would like to see new places and learn new things, but the older people in his life don't like his plan. They can only see problems. Chris finds that he, too, is a little afraid of change.

CHARACTERS IN THE PLAY

Chris, a young person who wants to travel

Cox
Mills
Harris   } five of Chris's friends, all older than him
Dean
Wright

PERFORMANCE NOTES

At the beginning of the play Chris's friends are in a room. Cox is reading a book, Mills and Harris are talking quietly to each other, and Wright and Dean are looking out of a window.

You will need six chairs, a book, a bag and a map.

Canada Can Wait

Cox, Mills and Harris are sitting in a room. Dean and Wright are standing by a window. Chris comes in.

CHRIS (*Smiling*) Well, goodbye, everyone.

COX (*Putting down his book*) Are you going?

CHRIS Yes, I must.

MILLS When are you going?

CHRIS Now.

'Well, goodbye, everyone.'

COX   Now? So soon?

MILLS   Don't go!

CHRIS   But I must. I need a change.

HARRIS   What are you going to do?

CHRIS   I'd like to travel for a time.

HARRIS   Travel? How wonderful!

DEAN   Yeah, think of us when you're travelling.

COX   Yes, think of us – we have to stay here.

MILLS   It's the same old thing, day after day—

HARRIS   The same old faces.

WRIGHT   The same old problems.

MILLS   Nothing different for us!

DEAN   But someone has to do it.

COX   Yes, that's right. We can't *all* go!

CHRIS   Why not? You can travel too.

COX   Us? (*He laughs.*)

MILLS   How can we travel?

HARRIS   We have things to do here.

CHRIS   What things?

WRIGHT   He says, 'What things?'

DEAN   What a question!

COX   (*To the others*) He's tired of us.

CHRIS   No, I'm not. I'm not tired of you. I'm happy here.

MILLS   Are you?

CHRIS   Well, I *was* happy here. It's a good place, and I—

HARRIS   Yes?

'Spain, perhaps, or Greece . . .'

CHRIS   Well, I like you. I'm one of you – one of the group.

WRIGHT   That's nice.

DEAN   So where would you like to go?

CHRIS   I don't know. Spain, perhaps, or Greece . . . maybe even Canada—

COX   Canada?

CHRIS   Yes. I'm very interested in Canada.

MILLS   Canada, well!

HARRIS   That's interesting.

WRIGHT   You're very adventurous, Chris.

COX   We're not adventurous at all, I'm afraid.

DEAN   But then you're young—

'The lakes and the forests . . .'

COX	You have your life in front of you.
MILLS	You want to see exciting places—
HARRIS	Like Canada!
WRIGHT	The lakes and the forests . . .
COX	The great St. Lawrence River . . .
DEAN	How wonderful!
COX	Lucky Chris!
MILLS	It's different for us. We have to stay here. We can't go to Canada.
HARRIS	'I'm one of you,' you said, 'one of the group.' But you're not!

DEAN   No, Chris, you're different from us—

CHRIS   No, I'm not! Stop talking like this. I'm not different from you. Sometimes I'm happy, sometimes I'm not. I work and eat and sleep, like you.

MILLS   Ah, but *you* are going away—

HARRIS And *we* are staying here.

WRIGHT And that makes you different.

CHRIS   I'm *not* different!

COX   But what about Canada?

CHRIS   Stop talking about Canada! I'm not going to Canada – I'd *like* to go there, that's all!

COX   So you *aren't* going there now?

CHRIS   I don't know. Perhaps. I need some time to think about my life.

WRIGHT Oh, yes.

DEAN   Everyone does.

MILLS   It's usual for people to do that.

HARRIS And there's lots of time. You're young.

CHRIS   That's right. I have my life in front of me.

HARRIS So, take your time.

CHRIS   Right.

WRIGHT You can stay here as long as you like—

DEAN   And think about it.

CHRIS   Yeah. (*He sits down.*)

ALL   Mmm . . .

Everyone is quiet for a moment.

COX   So what are you going to do?

CHRIS   Sorry?

MILLS   Are you leaving today?

CHRIS   Leaving? Er, not today. I want to think about it first.

MILLS   Of course.

HARRIS When are you going, then?

CHRIS   Well, not now. Later, perhaps. I can stay here a bit longer. There's lots of time. (*Laughing*) Canada can wait, can't it?

WRIGHT Yes, it can. It certainly can!

DEAN   You're one of us really, aren't you, one of the group?

CHRIS   Yes, I am, I think.

COX   (*Laughing*) But, you know, you say—

CHRIS   Yes? Say what?

COX   Well, you say some funny things sometimes!

CHRIS   Like what?

COX   Well, *Canada!*

Cox, Mills, Harris, Dean and Wright all laugh.

CHRIS   (*Looking at them*) What's so funny about that?

MILLS   (*Laughing quietly*) It doesn't matter.

HARRIS Forget it.

COX   Look at the time – I must go!

MILLS   Me too. I have a lot to do.

HARRIS And me.

WRIGHT   Let's all go.

DEAN   Yes, let's leave Chris with his dreams—

COX   About *Canada*!

They all laugh at Chris.

COX   See you later, Chris.

ALL   Bye-bye.

COX   (*To Chris*) Bye-bye, traveller!

Chris's friends laugh, and then go out. Chris stands and watches them go. He doesn't look happy. He opens his bag and takes out a large map. He opens the map on the floor and looks at it carefully.

CHRIS   Thailand . . . Malaysia . . . Indonesia . . . Australia . . . (*He looks up, smiling.*) Mmm, Australia!

'Mmm, Australia!'

INTRODUCTION

A man goes into a grocery store and buys a lot of salt. At first the other people in the store can't understand why. Then they hear his story, and they all want to buy salt too.

CHARACTERS IN THE PLAY

Shopkeeper, a person who owns a small grocery store

Groot
Nello
Durg
Spratly
} four people in the grocery store

Manra, a truck driver

PERFORMANCE NOTES

Scene 1: In a small grocery store.

Scene 2: In a street, some hours later.

You will need ten bags of salt, and a small cart on wheels. You will need the noise of a truck stopping suddenly, but we do not see the truck.

Salt

No more salt

In a small grocery store, Groot is asking the shopkeeper for something. The others are waiting behind him.

GROOT I'd like ten bags of salt, please.

SHOPKEEPER Ten? Of course. That's ten dollars, please.

GROOT Here you are.

SHOPKEEPER Can I help you with all that?

GROOT No, thanks. I have this cart.

SHOPKEEPER Ten bags. That's a lot of salt.

GROOT Yes. Salt is very important, you know.

SHOPKEEPER It is. But why do you need *ten* bags?

GROOT Soon there isn't going to be enough salt in the world. I saw it on television.

SHOPKEEPER Not enough salt? Really?

GROOT It's true. So I'm buying some now. Goodbye!

He goes out with his cart.

NELLO Did you hear that?

DURG Yeah, there isn't enough salt in the world.

SPRATLY Not enough salt? That isn't true.

NELLO But he saw it on television. Soon there isn't going to be any in the stores.

'Did you hear that?'

SPRATLY   Really? That's bad – I need salt.

DURG   Me too. I can't live without it!

NELLO   (*To the shopkeeper*) Give me some salt, please, ten bags – no, make that twenty bags.

SPRATLY   And me. I'd like thirty bags.

DURG   Me first! I've got a big family. We need salt.

SHOPKEEPER   Be quiet, all of you! You must wait.

NELLO   But we want our salt.

DURG   And we want it now.

SHOPKEEPER   But that man bought my last ten bags.

SPRATLY   Then it's true! He was right – there isn't enough salt in the world. What are we going to do?

SHOPKEEPER That's *your* problem. It's six o'clock – time to close the store. I'm going home.

NELLO But what about our salt?

SHOPKEEPER Look, there's a lot of salt in the world – enough for everybody. Goodbye!

They all go out.

Scene 2
We want salt!

Spratly finds Groot standing in a street with his cart.

SPRATLY Excuse me, I want to buy some salt.

GROOT Sorry? What did you say?

SPRATLY I know about the problem.

GROOT What problem? What are you talking about?

SPRATLY Soon there isn't going to be enough salt.

GROOT Oh, you heard about that?

SPRATLY Yes, and I want some salt.

GROOT Then go to a grocery store and buy some.

SPRATLY I can't find any. Every time I ask, the shopkeeper says, 'Sorry, no more salt.'

GROOT Oh dear!

SPRATLY But *you* have some. You bought ten large bags – I saw you.

GROOT I'm sorry, but I'm not selling my salt.

'But you *have* some.'

SPRATLY   But I'll give you ten dollars a bag.

GROOT   (*Laughing*) No, I want fifty dollars a bag! It's more expensive every day. Soon there isn't going to be enough.

SPRATLY   All right, all right, fifty dollars a bag! Give me five bags. Here's the money.

GROOT   Good man! You're doing the right thing.

Spratly goes out. Durg comes in.

DURG   Excuse me, I saw you buy some salt.

GROOT   Ah!

DURG   What's happening? I can't find any. The shopkeepers all say, 'Sorry. No more salt!'

GROOT   There's a problem.

DURG   I know. It was on television. Everybody is talking about it. Listen, I must have some salt.

GROOT   Sorry, I can't help you.

DURG   But I need it for my family. Please!

GROOT   All right, all right, but it's . . . er . . . a hundred dollars a bag.

DURG   Oh no!

GROOT   I told you – everybody wants salt. Well?

DURG   Oh, all right, then. Give me four bags.

GROOT   Four? Good! You understand the world, my friend. I see it in your face.

DURG   Here's the money.

GROOT   And here's your salt! Goodbye.

Durg goes out. Nello comes in.

NELLO   Hey, you, stop!

GROOT   Are you talking to me?

NELLO   Yes, you were in the grocery store—

GROOT   Was I? Perhaps. I go into a lot of grocery stores.

NELLO   You bought all the salt in the store!

GROOT   Well, there's a problem, you know.

NELLO   Yes, there is – and it's all because of you!

GROOT   That's not true!

NELLO   I met Spratly just now. He tried to sell me a bag of salt for five hundred dollars!

GROOT   That's too much.

NELLO Of course it is – I know your plan! You go from store to store. You buy all the salt, and sell it for a lot more money!

GROOT OK, it's true – I buy and sell salt – that's not wrong.

NELLO Then sell some to me.

GROOT No, I don't want to.

NELLO (*Holding him, angrily*) Listen, I'm going to buy, and you're going to sell. (*Shouting*) Do you understand?

GROOT But I've only got one bag left.

NELLO (*Angrily*) Give it to me, then!

GROOT It's two hundred dollars. Well, OK, you can have it for a hundred and fifty. But let me go!

NELLO (*Shouting*) Give it to me!

GROOT No, give me the money first. Now let me go! Oh, help! Help!

Groot runs out. We hear a truck stop suddenly, and Groot cries out. The driver, Manra, comes in, helping Groot to walk.

MANRA He ran in front of my truck. I didn't see—

NELLO You didn't do anything wrong. It was an accident.

MANRA But why did he run across the street without looking?

NELLO I was angry with him. So he ran away.

MANRA (*To Groot*) How do you feel?

'He ran in front of my truck.'

GROOT   (*Holding his leg*) Oh, my leg! My leg hurts. I think it's—

NELLO   He's OK, I think.

MANRA   Wait a minute, what's this in the street?

NELLO   It's salt. He had a bag of salt and I wanted it.

MANRA   Salt? Well, that's interesting! I'm carrying salt on my truck – bags and bags of it!

NELLO   Salt? Oh no! (*He laughs.*)

MANRA   Why are you laughing?

NELLO   It doesn't matter. I can't tell you now.

MANRA   Then you can tell that policeman. Look, he's coming across the street now. He saw the accident, I think!

31

INTRODUCTION

Maggie works in a fast-food restaurant. People come here to buy food when they haven't got much time. The restaurant sells 'fast food' – things like pizza, burgers, chicken and sandwiches. Five angry people are waiting for their food.

CHARACTERS IN THE PLAY

Maggie, a young woman who works in a fast-food restaurant

Two men } people who want to buy some food to eat
Three women }

PERFORMANCE NOTES

In the window there is a sign saying, 'Fast Food'. There are some tables and chairs, and a large high counter. Maggie is standing behind this counter. The people in the restaurant are standing in front of it. They are wearing outdoor clothes. Maggie is wearing work clothes. She also needs a bag.

Slow Food

MAN 1 Excuse me, is my food ready?

MAGGIE What did you ask for?

MAN 1 I asked for chicken.

MAGGIE Er, let's see. Another five minutes.

MAN 1 Five minutes?

MAGGIE Sorry, ten minutes.

MAN 1 Ten? That's no good! I must go back to my office in ten minutes.

MAN 2 And what about *my* food? I asked for a burger and French fries fifteen minutes ago!

'I asked for a burger and French fries fifteen minutes ago!'

MAGGIE I'm sorry, but there are a lot of people eating here today.

MAN 2 But how long is it going to take? My train leaves in forty minutes.

MAGGIE Not long. I'm very sorry.

WOMAN 1 Excuse me, I was before these men. Where is my coffee?

WOMAN 2 And what about me? I asked for a sandwich and a coke half an hour ago.

WOMAN 3 Well, I'm before all of you. I asked for a pizza forty-five minutes ago.

MAN 1 Look here, in your window it says, 'Fast food'.

MAGGIE Yes, it does.

MAN 1 Then why is it so slow?

MAGGIE It isn't slow. But people today want everything faster and faster—

MAN 1 What are you talking about?

WOMAN 1 Look, I can't wait. I have to get back to work.

WOMAN 2 And I have a meeting. I'm late.

MAN 2 Time is money, you know!

WOMAN 3 Where's my pizza?

WOMAN 1 Where's my coffee?

MAN 1 What about my chicken?

PEOPLE We want our food!

MAGGIE Please, everybody! Please! Your food is coming. He's doing it now.

'We want our food!'

PEOPLE *He?*

MAGGIE Sorry, *they*. The chefs are doing it now.

MAN 2 How many chefs have you got?

MAGGIE Oh, lots.

WOMAN 2 How many?

MAGGIE Some.

WOMAN 1 How many exactly? Tell us!

MAGGIE Er, twelve.

WOMAN 3 Your restaurant has twelve chefs?

MAGGIE Well, no, not now. We had one in January, one in
February, one in March – one every month for the
last year. That makes twelve.

WOMAN 3 Well, where are they now?

'Your restaurant has twelve chefs?'

MAGGIE   They all stopped working here.

WOMAN 1   Why did they leave?

MAGGIE   Because it was too fast for them.

MAN 2   And how many chefs have you got now?

MAGGIE   Well, er . . . one.

PEOPLE   One!

MAGGIE   No, sorry. That's wrong—

MAN 1   I'm happy to hear it!

MAGGIE   We haven't got *any*.

PEOPLE   What?

MAGGIE   That's right. There's only me here. Our last chef left yesterday. He was fed up with fast food.

MAN 2   Fed up?

MAGGIE Yes. He said to me, 'That's it! Enough! No more fast food for me! I'm going!' And he went.

WOMAN 2 But what about our—

MAGGIE And do you know? I'm fed up too. Yes, I'm really, really fed up. Fast chicken, fast burgers, fast French fries, fast coke, fast coffee, fast talking, fast walking, fast eating, fast sleeping, fast living, fast dying! I'm fed up with it all!

WOMAN 1 But who is going to—

MAGGIE What's the matter with everybody these days? Why is everything so fast? Come here. (*Maggie walks to the window.*) Come on! (*The people all go to the window.*) Look outside. Go on, look! It's a beautiful day. Life is beautiful. We can all be happy. But first we must slow down. We must take the time to *live*.

MAN 1 Live? But we have to work!

WOMAN 3 We have lots to do.

WOMAN 1 And we want food.

MAN 2 We want *fast* food—

WOMAN 1 Not *slow* food!

WOMAN 2 We haven't got time to—

MAGGIE Time! Time! Time! Don't talk to me about time. You don't understand it. You – oh, it's no good, you're not listening to me.

She takes off her work clothes and picks up a bag.

WOMAN 3   Hey, where are you going?

MAGGIE   I'm going out. I'm going to sit in the sun. I'm going to look at the sky and listen to the sea. I'm going to do nothing . . . *slowly*!

WOMAN 1   But what about our food?

MAN 2   What about my burger?

MAGGIE   *You* can do it!

MAN 2   *What* did you say?

MAGGIE   I said, you can do it. Behind me is the kitchen. In the kitchen there's a big bag of chicken and another bag of burgers. You can do your own food, and you can do it as fast as you like. Goodbye!

PEOPLE   But we don't—

MAGGIE   And have a nice day!

She goes out.

'We must take the time to live.'

EXERCISES

A Checking your understanding

1 *Choose the best question-word and answer these questions.*
   What   Who   Why
   1 . . . thinks of the plan to rob the bank?
   2 . . . is the matter with Michael Scott?
   3 . . . does Chris want to travel?
   4 . . . buys four bags of salt at a hundred dollars a bag?
   5 . . . does Maggie leave the restaurant in the end?

2 *Are these sentences true (T) or false (F)?*
   1 The woman working in the library is afraid of the robbers.
   2 The woman in blue wants to help the man lying in the street.
   3 The older people laugh at Chris and his dreams.
   4 In the end Chris wants to stay at home.
   5 Nello understands Groot's plan to buy all the salt.
   6 Maggie likes fast food.

3 *Who said these words, in which play, and about what?*
   1 'You're very adventurous.'
   2 'Oh, that's nice. They look interesting. Thanks.'
   3 'But how long is it going to take? My train leaves in forty minutes.'
   4 'Can I help you with all that?'
   5 'We helped someone famous.'
   6 'You just put your hand in your pocket like this.'
   7 'Well, you say some funny things sometimes!'
   8 'What does it say? Read it!'

B Working with language

1 *Put together these beginnings and endings of sentences from the five plays.*
  1 you must go into the bank
  2 I'm sorry, you can't borrow books
  3 yeah, think of us
  4 to think about my life.
  5 if you feel ill,
  6 without a library card.
  7 I need some time
  8 take one of these pills.
  9 when you're travelling.
  10 and you must speak to everyone there.

2 *Use these words to join the sentences together.*
  and   because   but   so   when
  1 The robbers didn't steal any money. They went into the wrong building.
  2 Patrick helped the man to sit up. He gave him some water.
  3 The people in the restaurant wanted fast food. Maggie couldn't help them.
  4 Chris began to feel happier. He looked at his map.
  5 Groot bought all the salt. He could get rich quickly.

C Activities

  1 Write Nello's conversation with the policeman about Groot's accident.
  2 Write a newspaper report to go with this headline:
  TV CHEF FOUND ILL IN STREET

D Project work

You are a student with a 'free' year and you can travel anywhere you like. Where do you want to go, and why? What places do you want to see there? What are you going to do there? What must you take with you?

GLOSSARY

adventurous of someone who likes doing exciting and dangerous things

asleep of someone who is sleeping; not awake

bank a place that keeps money safe for people

borrow to take and use something that you are going to give back after a short time

buy (past tense **bought**) to give money to get something

counter a long high table in a shop or a restaurant that is between the people who work there and the people who want to buy things

dream a hope for something nice in the future

fed up of someone who is not happy or who is bored because they have or do too much of something

funny of something that makes you laugh; of something that is not usual or is different

grocery store a building where people buy food and other small things for the home

group a number of people together

gun a thing that shoots out bullets to hurt or kill people

heart the thing inside the body that makes the blood go round

kneel down (past tense **knelt down**) to go down on your knees

library a place where you go to borrow or read books

library card a piece of plastic from a library with your name on it; you use it to borrow books

nurse a person who helps people who are sick or hurt

pill a small, round, hard medicine that you swallow

pizza a round, flat, Italian bread

plan something that you are going to do, and how you are going to do it

problem something that is difficult

restaurant a place where people buy food and eat it

rob to take things that are not yours from a bank, train (or other places) or people

robbery taking things that are not yours from a bank, train (or other places) or people

salt white stuff that comes from sea water; we put it on food to make it taste better

sell (past tense **sold**) to give something to somebody who pays you money for it

shoot (past tense **shot**) to send a bullet from a gun to hurt or kill someone

steal (past tense **stole**) to take something that is not yours

take (past tense **took**) **someone's pulse** to feel the beating of the heart in the wrist (or the neck)

travel to visit other countries

TV chef a person who cooks food on television

wake up to stop sleeping

world where we all live; people live in lots of different countries in the world